Fashion Coloring Book

For Adults, Teens, and Girls of All Ages

CREATIVE COLORING PRESS

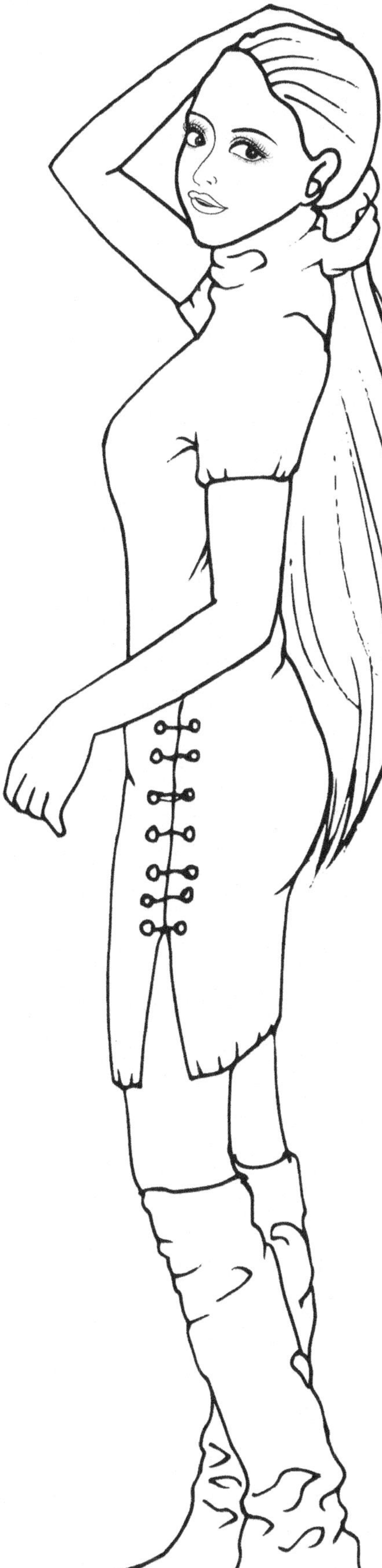

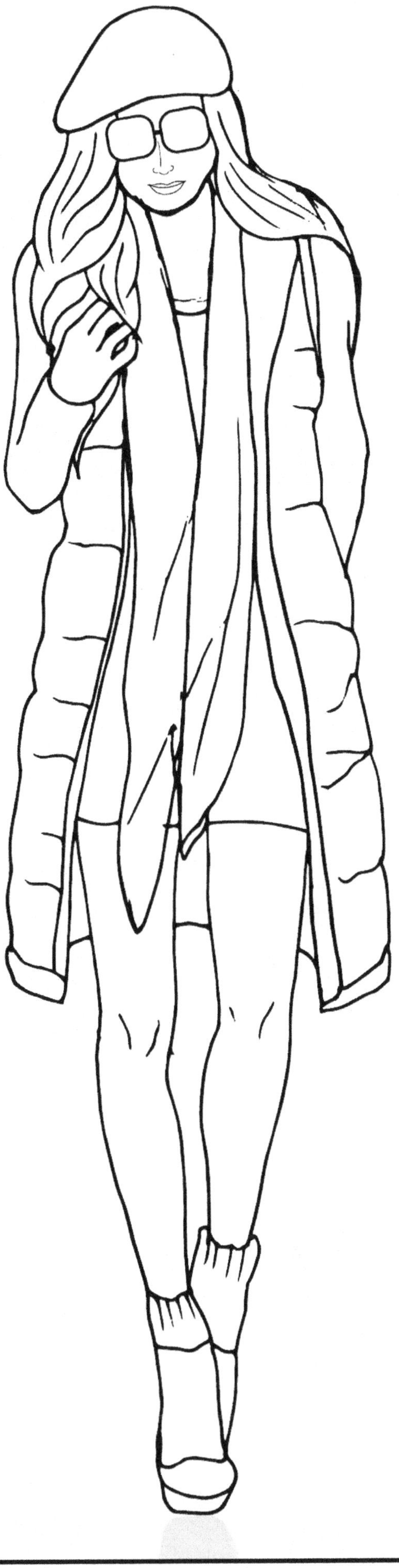

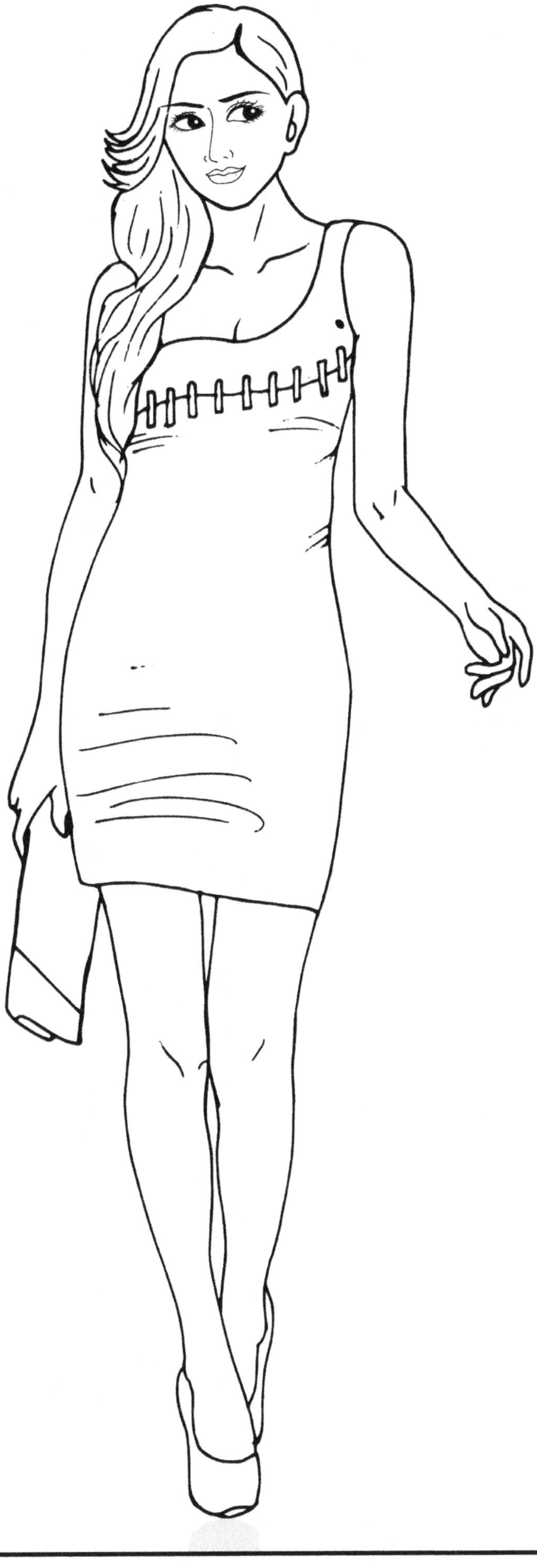

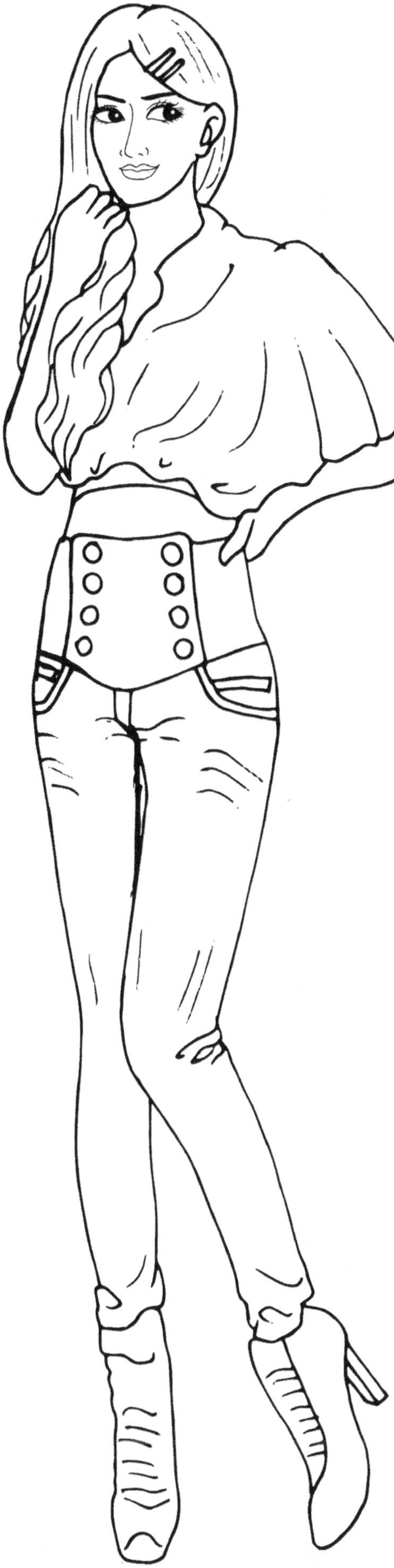

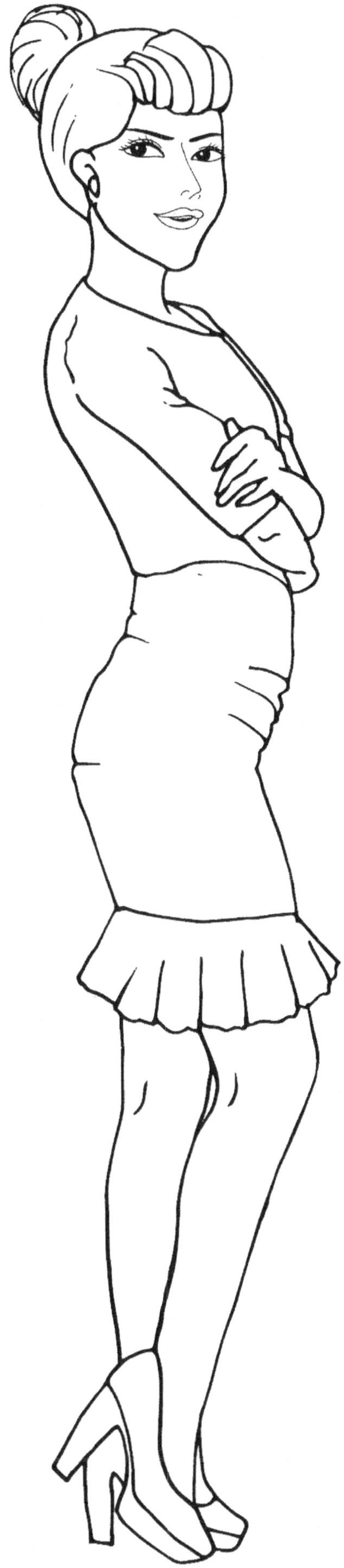

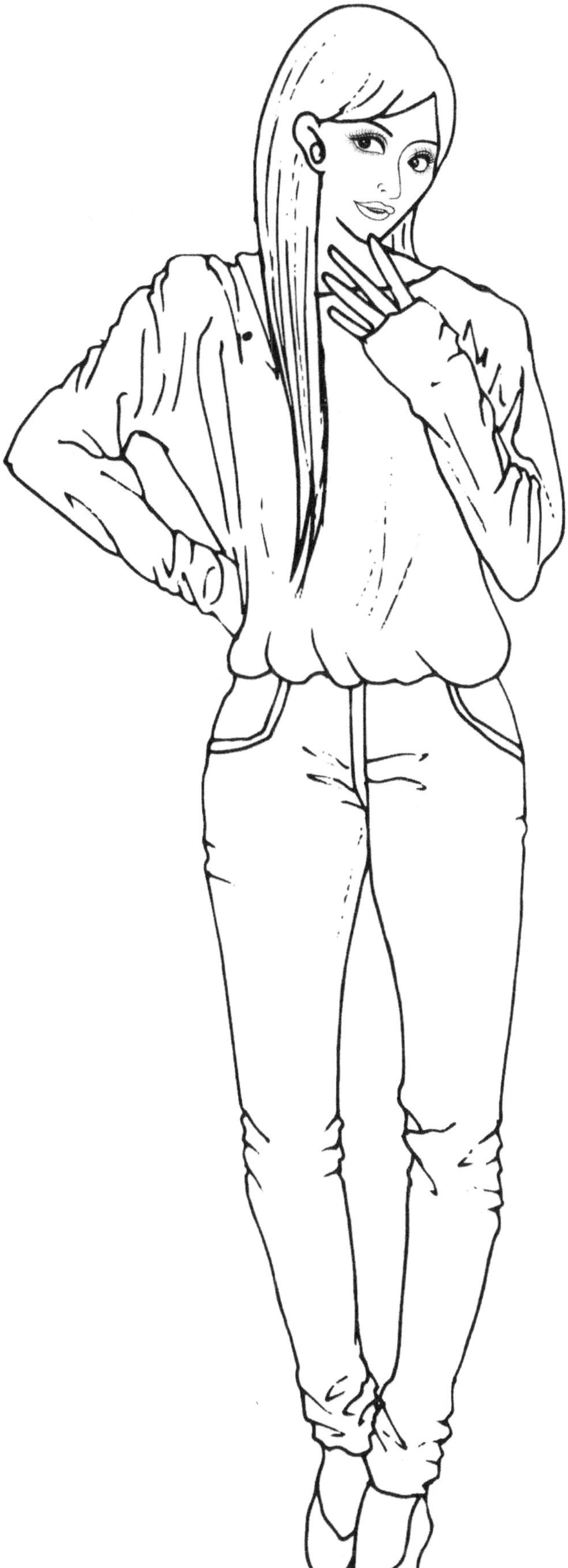

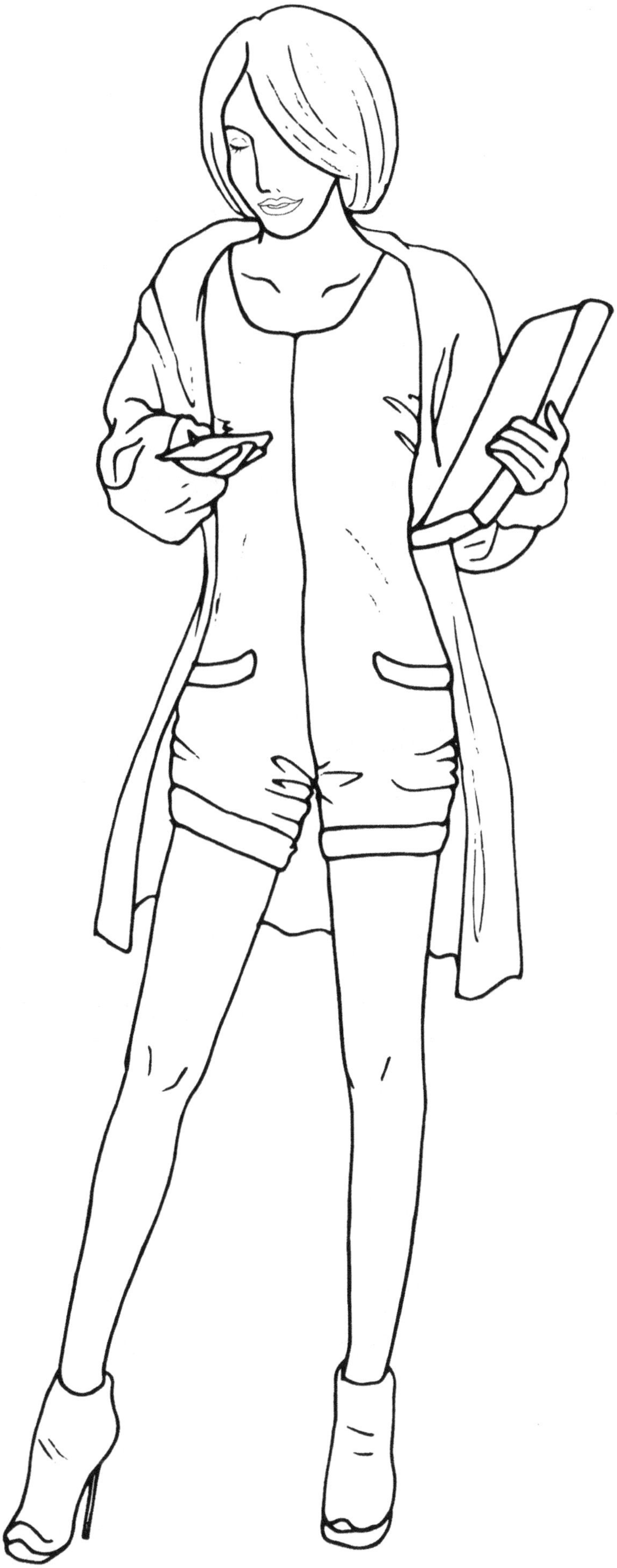

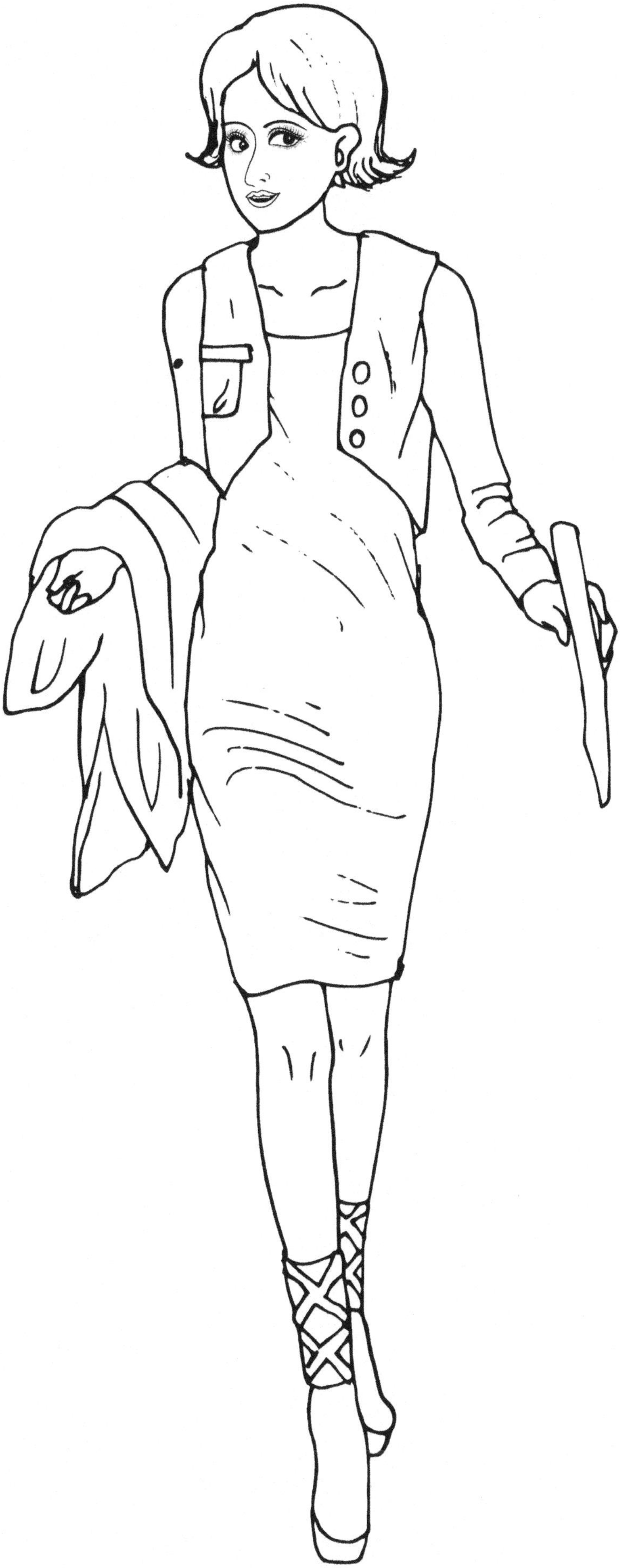

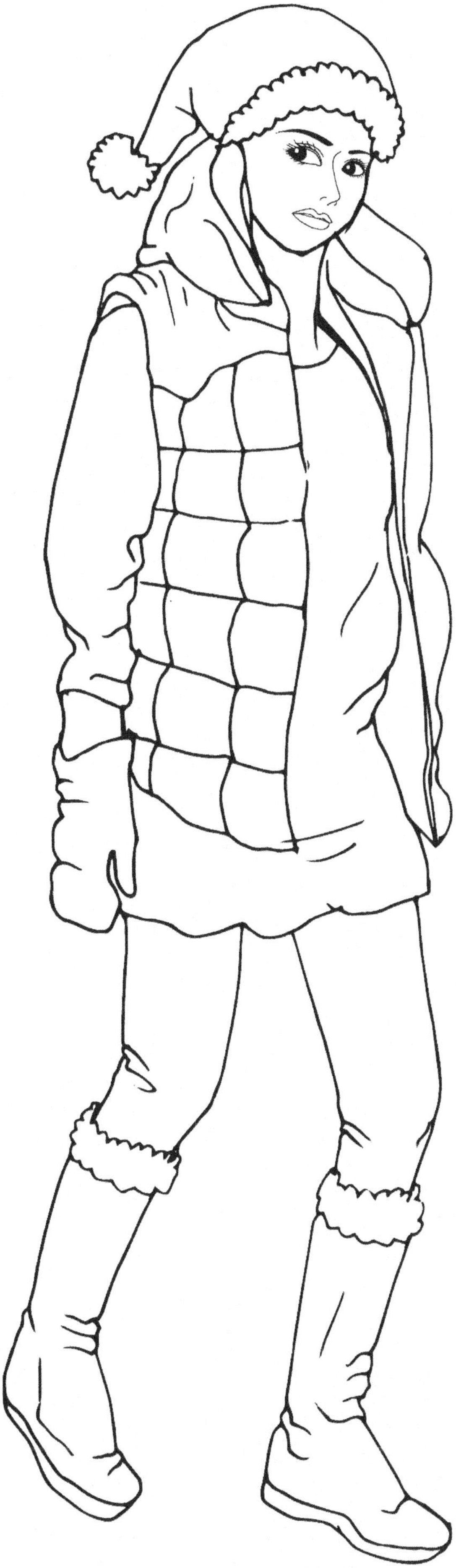

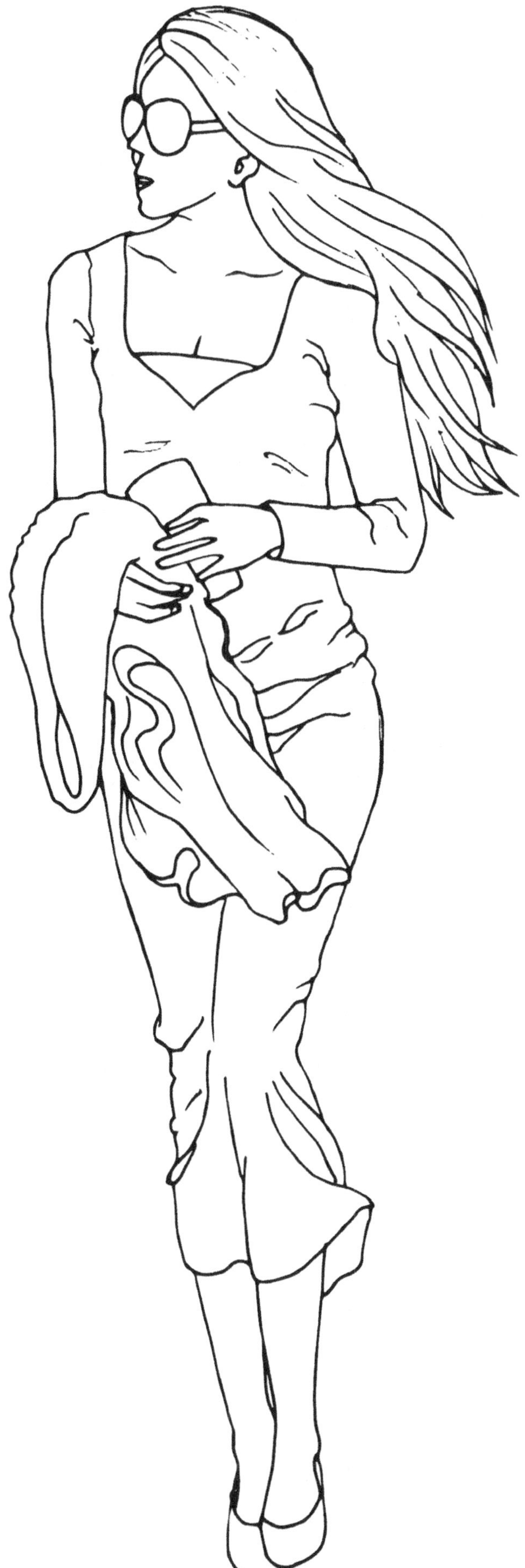

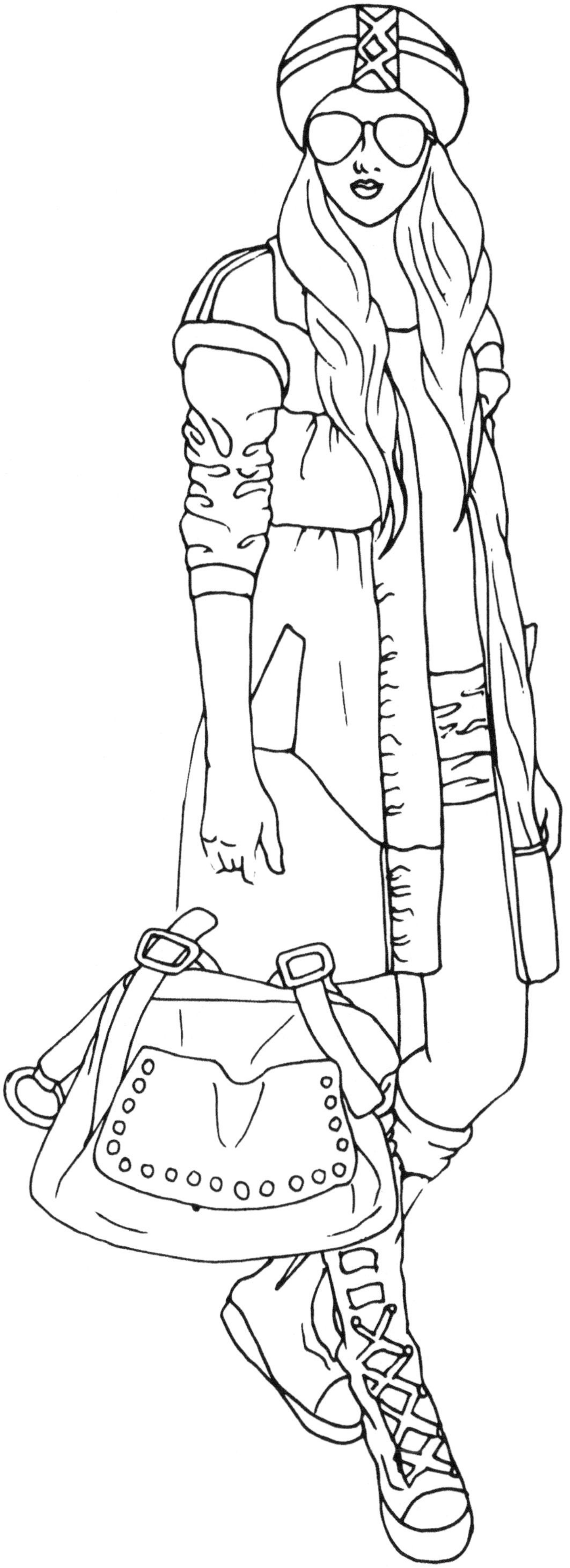

Made in the USA
Coppell, TX
20 April 2021

54207185R00046